A Primer for Buford

A Primer for Buford
WILMA ELIZABETH McDANIEL

Hanging Loose Press

Published by Hanging Loose Press
231 Wyckoff Street
Brooklyn, New York 11217

Cover art by Ann Mikolowski

Hanging Loose Press thanks the Literature Programs of the
New York State Council on the Arts and the National Endow-
ment for the Arts for funding in support of the publication
of this book.

Library of Congress Cataloging-in-Publication Data

McDaniel, Wilma Elizabeth.
   A primer for Buford.

     1. Oklahoma – Poetry. 2. Migrant labor – California –
Poetry. I. Title.
PS3563.A272P75   1989   811.54   89-26757
ISBN   0-914610-88-0
ISBN   0-914610-87-2 (pbk.)

 Produced at The Print Center., Inc., 225 Varick St.,
New York, NY 10014, a non-profit facility for literary
and arts-related publications. (212) 206-8465

Introduction

Young Buford will find no better mentor than Wilma Elizabeth McDaniel because no writer has more powerfully or more originally captured the lives of California's Okies. People who read *The Grapes of Wrath* can in her poems trace the Joads beyond that boxcar where the novel ended. Indeed, Wilma herself represents well the great contribution made – however unwillingly – to California.

She is no longer the awkward teenager who journeyed with her family from "Big Muddy," no indeed. Today she is a writer – humane, humorous and unflinching. Critic Cornelia Jessey praised her "dry and burning phraseology," and novelist James D. Houston called her work "absolutely unique and magical."

The first lines of the first poem in her first book, *The Carousel Would Haunt Me* –

> Mooney's Grove is in my blood
> like hemoglobin, I suppose
> that I would become anemic
> if the county barred me...
> (from "Mooney's Grove")

– revealed that an extraordinary vision and voice had been brewing in California's Great Central Valley where the poet has lived for fifty years. To that valley Wilma brought values honed elsewhere, values that have become part of what makes her region of the golden state unique.

Like Joe Fluty in "Essentials"– who

> ...didn't take anyone with him
> but a coondog
> and some scratchy records
>
> of Jimmie Rogers

– Wilma brought the core of rural Oklahoma to rural California. And, like Vonetta Jones in "Okie Teenage Girl Describes Friend, 1936," she also brought a talent:

> "I see color
> smell it
> taste it
> and take it home for my
> dreams."

True to place, true to people, yet powerfully universal, Wilma's language is as vernacular as what you might hear in a Central Valley shopping mall and her subjects are as palpable as breath itself.

Wilma's poetry offers remarkable folk wisdom, revelations of the intimate braiding of her two states, and glimpses of life lived on the cusp of poverty where hope and hopelessness dance. In fact, she has written here a primer not only for Buford, but for all of us.

Gerald Haslam
Penngrove, California

CONTENTS

Roster

Appearances

A PRIMER FOR BUFORD

Wilma Elizabeth McDaniel

ORIGINS

A PRIMER FOR BUFORD

Uncle Claudie Windham's life
has weathered to the color of
wisdom
only a few things bother him
now
mainly his grandson Buford Windham, Jr.

He laments
That boy ain't growing up right
in Berkeley where his mother teaches
I mean he don't know nothing
his daddy done
when he was a boy in Oklahoma

Why he don't even know our language
if you told him there was a roller
coming
he'd think you meant a steam roller

Uncle Claudie shakes his head
I reckon Buford needs a primer
like we had in the first grade
start from scratch
and learn where he come from

Pretty soon
there won't be anyone left that
can tell him

ORIGINS

By a still small voice

heard above the choking
winds

that had filled their mouths with
dust
instead of food

the Okies in California
always knew
where they had come from

VIA DOLOROSA

Dustbowl women
cried special tears

on the Highway 66
Exodus to California

yellow
from snubs and fever
abusive stateline guards

purple
when tires went flat
and the waterhose broke

YOU CAN'T GO BACK

Willis Cates told Papa
out in the plum orchard

Things have changed Mister Mac
since our move in 'thirty-five

Nothing is the same for me and
mine

Coming West
you can't go back

to where you was
even if you could get there

18

SURPRISE VISIT FROM CHILDHOOD
FRIEND TURNED BANKER

Harvey Wilcox
tracked me down
wearing his Stetson
and I love that

meanest kid
in our two-room school
carried a Tom Mix toy pistol
and shot everyone dead in
the fourth grade

You wouldn't believe
how far a country boy can go
with crock-cut hair
and dropseat pants

ESSENTIALS

PAPA BROADCASTING TURNIP SEED

He was a graceful
young man
with blue-glass eyes

he didn't know Greek
and he couldn't tell color

but he planted purple
all over the land

and told the tragedy of
Bud Kinchloe
by lantern light

PAPA AT THE PLOW

The sun came up with
his morning disposition

and nothing could unsmile
his smile, except the plow on
balky days

when the world was full of
rocks

and rows would end in
the Promised Land

Then he would curtain
off the sun
his own face

and long for barn dance
nights
when pomade glistened
on the young blades' hair

and fiddles waltzed him
"Over the Waves"

ROCKING HORSE

The price of cotton
was high that year
and Papa bought Buster
a rocking horse

and tied it to the tree
on Christmas Eve

Next day
Buster rocked on it
all around the world
to the Crib
where the Infant lay

and the bells rang out
in every town
peace on earth
to horse and rider
as they sped past

A GREEN GRAPE PIE

Athro Haley
had a gravel road up
to his house
and a full stomach

He stopped us four
walking proudly
home
with tin buckets of wild
grapes from the bottomland

and snorted
Green grapes is for possums
nothing fit for
pies

Hungry children
knew different:
green grapes
were full of promise

When we cut the crust
of Mama's supper pie
giant emeralds
spilled out on our cracked
plates

RED PEPPER SAUCE

Old Mister Jerrold lived
alone in Hog Hollow where
the post oak shade was deep

Papa tried to visit him
now and then, his Christian duty
Mama admonished

First visit Mister Jerrold confessed
Yes, I was married once
so many years ago
I can't even tell you what the girl
looked like
but I do remember she kept
red pepper sauce on the table
used it on everything

Took the bottle with her when she
left
anyway both of them were gone
when I came home from work
one evening

DOUBLE FRATRICIDE, 1923

Wade and Brently met at the
Holley pasture gate by
sheer accident
Wade was supposed to be
in Sapulpa that entire week
but everyone knew
both were carrying guns
already looking for
each other

WHOOPING COUGH EPIDEMIC, 1924

The preacher's wife curled
paper roses
and put them inside a glass
fruit jar

to decorate little Cora's grave
that frozen winter
of the township innocents

She went back in spring
and put a penny doll inside
the jar

to look out at the robins

PROPHETESS OF BIG MUDDY, 1925

Grandma Meade cut
a fourth mincemeat pie
out in the Christmas kitchen
listening to the chatter in
the living-dining room
It's too good to last
she predicted
A day like this will bring
us sorrow
you mark my words
the old *will*
and the young *may* die
it's Scripture
and she called, Who else
wants pecan pie
three pieces left

AMAZING GRACE

The summer doors
were wide open
Buster sat between
Mama and the Preacher's
wife
his overalls were new
his bare feet dangled

someone started clapping in
the back of the church
the choir began to sing

Amazing Grace, How Sweet the Sound
and Buster wondered what
that meant:
sugar was sweet
and honey too

but he guessed he'd never tasted
grace

TIMING

Only four years old
Uncle Bailey's twin boys
caught measles and whooping cough

Chub died after five days
with Doc Copley sitting beside
his bed
and him the healthy twin

but Pick
short for tootpick
lay on the cot with his hand
stretched out
on their old collie's head

and lived to die in the
Battle of the Bulge

PEEP SHOW FOR COUNTRY CHILDREN

Broken windows
sagging blinds

dusty yard
with dozing dogs:
never opened their eyes when
a phonograph scratched out

Let the Midnight Special Shine Her Lights on Me

and through a knothole
in the wall
we saw Evie Coulter

fifteen now
Tangee red in her blood

paint Clara Bow on her mouth
and dance the Charleston

ULYSSES IN OKLAHOMA

That sharecrop boy
should have plugged his
ears with cotton
from the twelve-foot sack
he dragged behind him

and never listened to the
siren song
of a country Lorelei
floating across Big Muddy

My Darling
You Can't Love But One
And Have Any Fun

should never
have followed the song to
its source

a honeyvoiced girl
who lived on the dark
side of the river

UNCLE EBBIE'S BACHELOR HOME IN THE HOLLOW

Featherbed high
his iron bed
had long round legs
showed off his army
blanket

a drape above
the curved white hip
of a chamberpot

BROTHER AND SISTER ON ERRAND

A rain crow made its melancholy
sound
somewhere deep in the recesses of
Oklahoma blackjacks. Their shade
covered us for one mile through
Barker's pasture. Our only visible
companion
was a long blacksnake that slithered
across the trees
over our heads. It glistened in a
penetrating ray of sunlight. Little Quill
stopped in the wagon-rutted road
and proclaimed
That there is a blue racer for sure. Some
say them things ain't poison
but one of them chased old man Watt's dog
and bit him on the nose.
Swelled up something fierce.

I tell you, Wanda
you cain't trust no snake.

REMEMBERING A CAT'S FUNERAL, 1926

My brother Harol
could walk on water
and knew protocol at
seven

he put tissue paper
over a comb
and played a dirge for
Andrew Jackson

led the cortege up
Post Oak Hill

where we laid poor Andrew
down in a crackerbox

DEACON HOSEA PHILPOT

Hosea wore stringties
and always carried
a Bible

went around singing
This Train Don't Carry No
Gamblers
No Drunkards
No Midnight Ramblers

Secretly
he went with a girl
from Bowlegs
who smoked
Lucky Strike cigarettes
and wore red garters

LITTLE EVA'S FUNERAL

Model T's lined the road
to Fairhaven Cemetery
Inside the gates
so many black dresses
so many serge suits

Wanda and Quill
hung back
and held each other's hand

over there against
the post oak trees
they saw the shovels

and now tears falling
into white handkerchiefs

REALITY

Silver foil
from chewing gum
made stars for our
Christmas tree
we hung paperchains on it
and strings of popcorn

Quill would work
a kernel loose
each time he passed
and pinch a lumpy parcel
marked with his name

This one here, he said
feels like longjohn underwear
it sure enough
ain't no toy

HAP TURNER'S LANTERN

His lantern hung in
the log granary
for seven years

flecked with imaginary blood
until someone carried it off
That much I know

But we heard some other stories
some lies, some true
of parties while the whiskey-
still operated full steam

and his Cajun wife Eulalia
danced with a rose between
her teeth

CONFRONTATION

Acid tongued Pellus told
his rustic son
You're gettin' too smart
for your age

and all Lex had said was
I want me a pair of waistpants
I'm gettin' too big to wear these
overhalls
when we go to town on Saturday

THE INTERPRETER

Newly moved to Big Muddy
pretty girl
big for twelve

and I didn't know that Molly
couldn't read the newspapers
on our sharecrop walls

until she pointed at Gary Cooper
and asked me
What do they say about him
ain't he good looking

AUNT SULA'S GOING AWAY PRESENT

Neighbor women made
her a quilt called Little Britches
comical pants
all over the bed
Proper pattern for you
they said, Britches
all them boys
thought you'd never get
your girl
and remember us now
and then
when you reach California

A MOTHER IN BIG MUDDY

Myella Foley
told things straight
and backed her tongue with
a razorstrap

when folks were pulling up
stakes she confronted her daughter:

Doreen
you don't go no place
with no man
that ain't your husband

to Californy
ner no place else
you're still fourteen
remember

and this here hag is your
mother

POLITICAL PHILOSOPHY, WINTER OF 1931

Aunt Flossie Bates lived
down in Wild Hog Hollow
read newspapers
and smoked Bull Durham
rolled her own

Always interested in politics
she reflected on the candidates
for the next year's election

Roosevelt
I haven't heard that name
much
since the days of Teddy and his
Roughriders

She stretched out her legs in
men's wool socks
and asked the kinfolks
eating popcorn around
the fire

When has the U.S. government
done anything for poor people?
I don't know why I bother to vote

She took a long drag on her
cigarette
and blew perfect smoke rings

But I aim to vote anyway
if things get better for women
it will be brought to pass by
women

SCOUTING WITH PLAYMATES, 1932

Five of us children
looking for black walnuts
found a cave
east of Big Muddy
We saw a bed of leaves
and Loftus being ten
said This here is a fox's den
as sure as you are born

We asked him
How do you know that

Can't you see them red hairs
where he has rubbed 'em off

Little Quill challenged him,
You don't know
everything in this world
Them red hairs could be from
Ballard's old egg-sucking dog

CONVERSATION, 1932

Mister Calhoun read a lot
more than most in Big Muddy

told my Uncle John
It's manifest destiny, that's
what it is
People hankering to push
on West
and conquer this land
or what's left
It's driving them, I tell you

Uncle John spat tobacco
More like starvation
driving them
I'd say, Mister Calhoun

AFTER OUR NEIGHBORS LEFT, 1933

Little Buster looked at
the empty house
and said

Don't them windows look
sad
like they was crying
because Mister Ferris
had to go to California
and take his kids

and he picked up
an old Prince Albert tobacco can
for a souvenir

FARM CHILDREN IN THE GRIP OF 1933

Coffee was grounds
flour was gone
cornmeal low
and fatback only a rind
February wind was ice
F.D.R. was a brand new voice

And we children played
a deadly game
each took a turn
at jumping off the top of the world
from a chicken house
calling
catch me
O-K-L-A-H-O-M-A
and didn't know why
we blamed our state

ESSENTIALS

Joe Fluty had an old
Model A
that he called Ruby Keeler

and he loaded up and
left for California

didn't take anyone with him
but a coondog
and some scratchy records

of Jimmy Rogers

AMERICAN
FOLK MUSIC,
1937

DUSTBOWL DOXOLOGY

Sweet
it was
is now
and ever shall be sweet
in memory
of wild walnut trees
at the spot
where curving banks
hugged
the faithful Merced River
and the sound of young
Sunday picnic voices
drifted downstream

GREAT DEPRESSION DEVOTIONS

Poor people had to guard
their faces
and hide their souls in the
Depression year of 1934

You couldn't tell a Catholic
from a Rosicrucian in the bread line
Who asked what someone believed
all held the creed
He who does not work
shall not eat
because he cannot find a job

But faith does not die easily:
buried like a bone for a starving
time
it burst out the day
Our Lady came to the packing shed
in a plain blue dress
stood in the midst of the sweaty
workers
and blessed them with loving
eyes

TO THE POINT

Hovis wore
a big black hat
pure Okie style
and him fourteen

The shed boss teased
Boy
did you steal your
daddy's hat

No sir
I worked all week
and bought me one

PICNIC TRAGEDY, 1934

Mexican Joe
stood on the shore
and held the baby and
diaper bag
while his wife and her
sisters rowed away

no one could swim
no one believed that they all
would drown
before Joe's eyes

while the valley sun
burned Lake McClure

OKIE TEENAGE GIRL DESCRIBES FRIEND, 1936

Crazy girl
that Vonetta Jones
talking poetry all the time
good sense, too
but don't make sense

talking how the packing shed
smells in peach and apricot
season
she grabs both her shoulders
and recites a poem
hers
It's all gold
and pink red roses

and hugs me when
we drive to Puccinello's

"I see color
smell it
taste it
and take it home for my
dreams"

OKIE BOY BOSS AT PUCCINELLO'S, 1936

The owner made him
shed boss at eighteen

tall
and thin
with Choctaw-color
eyes

he wore a planter's hat
and jeans
instead of overalls

Class
that's what he's got
I heard Beulah say
as Johnny Trueblood passed
with a box of peaches

It's a lot of things
that ring he wears
the way he walks
like he was gonna pounce
on someone any second

ABDICATION DAY

Uncle Bartis said to
us in the cold fog
of California 1936

If I was a king
you can bet
I wouldn't give up no throne
for a woman like
Mrs. Simpson

REVIVAL

Three tall brothers
Floyd
Bill
and Ruford Conley
stood up in the revival
clapped their hands
stamped their feet
and sang I've Got a Little Light
I'm Gonna Let It Shine

looked sideways at an Okie girl
with yellow hair
I've Got a Little Light
I'm Gonna Let It Shine

but the girl snapped her gum
and looked away

PICKING GRAPES 1937

Magic seventeen
and new in California

working in bursting
sweet vineyards

hot sand on soul
one strap held by a
safety pin

a girl could be whatever
she desired

the first breath of
Eve in Paradise

the last gasp of Jean Harlow
in Hollywood

REMEMBERING AN EVENT FROM 1937

Lila Faye Palmer bought
a bathing suit in Merced
couldn't swim a stroke
but jumped in an irrigation ditch
showing off her figure
if it hadn't been for Johnny Freitas
she'd have drowned for certain

that Portugee boy jumped in dressed
and saved her life
and carried her home to her mother
and married her two years later

NAMESAKE

Virgil and Leona Way lived
in an SP boxcar by the
old winery
and loved baseball

If anything
Leona was crazier than
Virgil about the game
When they had a baby
which Doc said was a
pure miracle

Leona named him Dean
for old "Diz" himself
and that pleased Virgil

he told her in the maternity
ward of the county hospital
I never liked my name nohow
and I brought you this rose

BASS FAMILY AT MIGRANT CREEK

Urbano had never heard of
Listerine mouthwash
he always smelled of garlic
cheap wine
and mammoth dreams—
very strong today

he knocked on the door
and told Ladonna
You leave the lights on and keep
the office open for me
and you won't have to pay
no rent this summer

Big deal Urbano
and you will stick me
with the electric bill
when you come back
from fishing

HIRED GIRL'S PET

Five a.m.
hens still drooped
half asleep on their perch
dreaming of fat cabbage worms
when Clara's rooster
the ravenous one
crowed the world awake for breakfast
Clara called him hers anyway
since the lady of the house
gave her a fertile egg and marked it with an X
unsmiling said
If this here egg hatches the chicken belongs to you
and kept her word
which was only fair

a hired girl
should have something that belongs to her
besides a patchwork quilt
she carries from job to job

STRATEGY

Stella was an Okie girl
with big green eyes
and wild red hair

stung by a wasp in the vineyard
she swore to us friends
Picking grapes is not for me
I gotta go somewhere else

and she saved her money
in a brown teapot that had
no lid
a penny
nickel
a now and then dime
month by month
until she bought a Greyhound
ticket
to Oakland, California

going up the bus steps
she called back
I don't ever want to pick an-
other grape again

THEM CHINAMEN HAS GOT A LOTTERY

Only eight years old
Bobby Gene was a tattletale
told everything he heard
like the time
he rushed in out of breath
and gasped

Harvey and Lowell played the
lottery
and won seven dollars
I ain't lyin' to you
them Chinamen has got a lottery
in Merced

right back of where we eat
the noodles
at Sing Lum's Rice Bowl

Oncet I peeked behind the
curtains
and seen 'em wearin' funny
robes

THE STORYTELLERS

Mr. Crowley is going back to school,
to finish his teach credential. He said,
"You people from Oklahoma are superb story-
tellers. I have never seen your equal. I
mean I have never heard your equal. I want
my two children to come over and just sit
out under the trees and listen to you talk.
I am desperately afraid that they will
grow up without the touch of magic so many
of you possess."

A SUMMER DATE

The Ginger Rogers moon was
only one chimney above the
Barkers' house

and the dance only begun
when Modena ran home
in her long voile dress

and jerked off the Woolworth
beads
Johnny Purvis gave to her at
Christmas

She sobbed out Daddy
I hate dancing
and I'll never go to the
Eagles Hall again

with Johnny Purvis
or any other boy

AMERICAN FOLK MUSIC, 1937

Fiddles fiddled
guitars strummed
pianos tinned
My Rose of San Antone
Bob Wills swing
O beat it out Leon

If Arlie Jones missed
a dance that summer
it broke his heart
until the next Saturday night

new shirt
ice cream pants
white shoes
and brilliantine on his hair

a waltz caught him up
and he danced with a girl
he'd never seen before

She smelled of rose talcum
and chewing gum
and they circled the floor
of sawdust dreams
to the refreshment stand

I'm crazy about Bob Wills'
music
the girl confided
with a coke bottle in her
hand
Makes you think you're
in another world

MY ROOM AT AUNT EURA'S, 1937

Working for school clothes
that Del Monte cannery summer
room and boarding
I slept in an iron bed with a faded
chenille spread
and saw sixteen years in a cracked
mirror
blistered cut and taped hands
dead tired feet
the bare walls welcomed me at night
breeze stirred the flimsy curtains
and brought the Man in the Moon
to my window
taunting me Borrow Jean Harlow's
evening gown
she will never miss it anyway
put on her slippers
come out and dance
I tossed
and turned to the wall where the
calendar hung
then fell asleep
and never heard the fishermen
come home from Pismo Beach

ROSTER

ROSTER

No alternative route
only one road leads from
yesterday

and every town
I pass through

is a place where someone
I have loved
died much too young

Merced
Fresno
and Malibu, California
Medford, Oregon
and El Paso, Texas

heaven forbid that
I should ever stop in
Boise, Idaho

Coda:
This is not a poem.
It is a cold fact.
Five of my brothers.
All young.

DAY OF RETURN, AUGUST 4, 1986

Bakersfield August
and its heat is modified hell
radio music has already begun to
stomp on me with fancy alligator
boots
everyone seems to have a cousin in
Kuzz
but it is good to be back in watermelon
country

a roadside stand reads Texas sweet
rattlesnake melons
plums 4 pounds for a dollar
cukes and stringbeans reasonable

entire new town
trying to hide its old roustabout
cotton picking past from me
high rise high price condominiums
occupants are not aware that I knew

their fathers and mothers
brothers and sisters
aunts and uncles at the end
of a long sharp hoe
shared many a tepid drink of
water from a wet burlap covered
jug

EXPLANATION

Orville Walker explains
Time caught up with me
and I wanted to retire with
homefolks
listen to the whippoorwills
at twilight
so I moved back to Tulsa
but Lord a mercy
everyone I ever knowed is
dead
or livin here in California

and them Oklahoma builders
haven't left no trees
or space for whippoorwills
to whip poor Will
and even though I cussed this
heat and tractor dust
when I was young

two thousand miles away from it
I missed the whole kaboodle

AFTER DEVALYN'S WEDDING

Lester told Grandpa Wiley, trying
to restrain his frustration behind
a ridiculous tight cummerbund

Papa, you embarrassed the hell out
of Devalyn
comin' in to the church tonight wearin'
your Stetson
and chompin' on a big cigar
not to mention her mother and me

Seems like we been workin' all our married
life
to give our girl a decent wedding
now don't look like I hit you with a two
by four
I reckon we'll live over it, but I'm sure
glad we don't have but one daughter

Let's go out to the kitchen and have ourselves
a piece of wedding cake
I was too keyed up to eat at the reception

I need coffee bad, I'd even drink a shot
of whiskey
if my blood pressure would take it

But it won't, Grandpa told him
stick to coffee, son

PROGRESS

Melvin stared at the
table centerpiece
and reflected to his
Bull Durham father

Ain't this something, Papa
five years in California
and we have went
from fresh fruit on our
table
to wax apples in a bowl

VARIETIES OF JAM

You hardly ever meet
a woman nowadays who can
make red pepper jam

or will lend you an old
clonker pickup
when your new lemon
goes dead in front of her
tarpapered shack

Women like Ocella Newby are
scarce
and no one west of
Plainview, Texas has the recipe
for that sweet hot jam

FLAWED VISION

Zona had magic eyes
coon-eyed round
and blue as a willow plate

She foresaw the future in
a crystal ball
that hung around her skinny
neck

every glorious day and night
of it
and heard the music calling

everything
except the scene where she was
fired
from Sears Roebuck

for doing Salome's dance in the
ladieswear department
instead of marking prices on
winter clothes

FAMILY BUSINESS

Carl Weyman and his
new wedding band wife
bought an old truck

instead of going on their
honeymoon

and started a huckster's
route from Modesto

first it was watermelons
late peaches
then sweet potatoes

after two years
two centuries they were
to Lynette
she went home to Texas

and Carl graduated into
shoe laces
liniment
and chalk dolls
bought a used tire for the
truck

PRIORITIES

Old Bill explained, My
new choppers don't fit nothing
but a cup on the shelf

when we found him on his
back porch
eating a big hard apple
with no teeth whatsoever

How do you do it, we asked
Got good gums, he answered
I eat fried rabbit, corn on the cob
anything that suits me

Teeth don't matter all that much
unless you are trying to get
another woman
or something like that

RESTRAINT ON HEARING NEWS OF H.R.

Although there are
deep creases
in the brow of the woman
in the mirror

if she could sing
she would be trilling
now

if she could dance
she would be tripping
this minute

as it is
she only removes curlers
from her hair
and reaches for a brush

ANGELIC PERSPECTIVE

Nothing
absolutely nothing can
shake Cynell Worthy's faith in life
since her Volvo sailed over the
bridge at White River
and landed on its wheels
with her unscathed

Small things
no longer bother her
a spot of bleach
dropped on a new pair of jeans

Cynell irons a strawberry
decal
onto the offending spot
singing
I'm gonna make it to heaven
I already
know how to fly

I DIDN'T COME HERE TO PITCH
NO HORSESHOES

The acrid smoke of charcoal fire drifts across
Murray Park. The aroma of barbecued ribs is heavy
in the Sycamore section. The Okie picnic has
reached its apex. Everyone is sated with food. One
short man works himself up from the table. His
paunch hangs over his belt. He proclaims, "Well,
the picnic is over when I cain't eat no more." He
defends his satement to the people still at the table.
"Ain't that the truth? Take all the good eats out
of a picnic, and what do you have left? Games?
I didn't come out here to pitch no horseshoes, too
much like hard work."

AUGUST 20, 1986

San Joaquin Valley seared
forty years ago
Papa died on a Prince Albert
Stetson hat
cowboy boots day like this

Nothing to take out of this
world
except a string of hearts

APPEARANCES

THE LONG WAIT

Entering town
from either direction, a billboard announces
Tulare, The City With A Smile
I cannot agree and do not smile

This town is grim
flat
pure sand
and ugly in color when you take a hard
look at it

Searching for one good feature in summer
you have to wait half a lifetime
until 110 degree heat has melted asphalt
burned out swamp coolers
ruined marriages that were
the least bit shaky
then cooled into Tule fog
until next April Fools' Day

GENE PETRELLI, VALLEY THESPIAN

He drove tractor
through the orchard all day
rehearsing his lines
from The Mousetrap
pulling boxes to the shed

came home at six
showered off the peach fuzz
ate a bowl of minestrone
still rehearsing his lines
on the way to the Playhouse

Four curtain calls
thunderous applause for
Gene as the Sergeant

a neighbor asked
why isn't your family here

Gene shrugged
I've gotta take this makeup off
and couldn't answer to himself

FATHERLY ADVICE

Uncle Claudie never talked
much about women to
Claudie Jr.
before he married a girl from
Mill Valley

all he said was, Respect women
always treat 'em good, son
even if they do things you don't
like

Remember that the best man
in the world
will never be as good as
a woman

Don't ask me why that is
but I know it's true

WORRIES OF A RURAL MOTHER

R.C. never sat down when
he drank morning coffee

but walked around in
a satin robe

with a dragon on the back

and plotted the day by
telephone

worried his Kansas mother
when she visited him in
California

No man in our family
ever wore a satin robe

even when he was sick
R.C. can't be thinking straight

a flannel robe would be
best for him

and a wife with a down-home
face

YOUR MONEY WILL BE REFUNDED

Cousin Lonza came home
upset in August heat
and threw his straw-hat on
the coffee table

Merle has cancelled out
he ain't comin' to the fair

Lonza's long face dropped farther
Nobody else can sing like him
something bad wrong with that
boy
and I wouldn't pay a nickel to hear
nobody else

FRONIE HAS LOST THE WAR

In light skirmishes
or heavy battle
jewelry has always been your
Waterloo
dear dumbbell Fronie
emeralds certified
genuine soda bottle glass

your ruby earrings
are red gumballs
fluke from a Kiwanis Club
machine

when you dropped your
last two quarters in
and turned the handle
twice

but war is always with us
and you gird up
and move on to other arenas
fake diamond strikes
bonanzas of pure gold
that will turn green tomorrow

VISITING ROMPERS COOLEY AGAIN

As a baby in French Camp
he wore those cute little
pants like his father wore
and folks still call him
Rompers

A whimsical boy
now gangling twelve
I remember when he
stuck his head inside
a picture frame
and called
Hang me on the wall

WATCHING TRUCK DRIVERS AT PANCAKE HOUSE

Boys
I always order pancakes
he told his buddies
slathered butter on them
poured syrup
like thick maple rain
Nothing much a cook
can do to ruin a pancake
if the stove don't blow up

PROFESSIONAL OPINION

In an empty room
with two folding chairs

I once served tea on
a cardboard box

to an architect
with a sweet tooth

who smoothed his
side of the box

and said
These lines are lovely

a useful piece
a holy item

and then he asked me
for another piece of cake

EMPTYING THE WASTEBASKET

My nephew
holed up in the bathroom
and wrote some stuff
on memo pads

that nearly knocked me down
when I emptied the wastebasket

"What good is one man"
he wrote

"Who weeps over little
battered kids
and never will
make any money

and won't be remembered
the day after his funeral"

and the boy is only fifteen

MISNOMERS

Names are idyllic on Cottonwood Road
Estrellita Cantina
can you believe that is the name of a dirty
tough bar
where Humberto Vega was gunned down
while mariachi music blared
La Paloma
and it turned out to be a case of mistaken
identity
the musicians were singing Cielito Lindo
very softly
when the sheriff and coroner arrived.

LAST COMMANDMENT

It was ironic that Mrs. Cooley
spent her last days
in a high-rise hospital
without one blade of grass
beneath her feet
or single cowbell tinkle from
the pasture
family crowded around her
hospital bed
that last day waiting for her
final breath
she could not hear, they thought

or speak a word
but at five-thirty sharp
suppertime on the farm
she opened her lips and demanded
of her daughter

"Maggie
Don't sell my churn"

APPEARANCES

Arfus Polk once asked
me out of the blue

What do you think
Jesus looks like

and when my face went
stone blank

Well, don't you
have no idea about
Him
at all, woman

K-MART SAGE

Dirty Stetson
khaki clothes
cane beside him
on a K-mart bench
I heard the old man say

you know
us men don't have to
look no certain way

like a woman does
or men expect her to look

you take Buck Owens
why he looks just right

if you put that face on
a woman
they'd run her out of town

WINGS

CONVERSION AND BAPTISM OF A BIKER

The event had been expected for
over a year
Jonathan came into the
rectory faithfully for instructions
now the day had arrived

His friends in black leather jackets
came by the dozen

They couldn't understand what was
taking place
though they stood reverently by the font

One whispered to another
Did you hear that?
Why do they call this a death?

THE STAMP

Waiting at the stop sign
I study faces
you there in the pale gray Lincoln with
hair and shirt that almost match

the color of your car
everything screams money

Another car pulls up and stops
someone rolls down a window
and calls to you, Knucklehead

You roll down yours and call
back to him,
Clint, old boy
when did they turn you loose
from the Mayo Clinic?

I heard Oklahoma in that voice
not Texas not Arkansas but Oklahoma
maybe from the town of Anadarko

The light turned green
the other car shot forward
Silverhead called after it
You come and see us, boy

TENANT IN NUMBER 14

Mr. Dobbs is frail
and chalky-white

like an ascetic monk
who forgot to wear his
habit

and put on someone else's
shirt and trousers

and a planter's hat
to do his marketing

Carrying a bag from Safeway
head bent
his lips are moving

perhaps he is reciting his
office

maybe only grumbling
about the price of food

SUMMER SCENE

July's turned its heat
up to broiling
feet are bare – dress is
minimal
grapes are oozing
and the Armenian Pope
has come to Fresno

WATERMELON BIN AT MARKET, JULY 4TH, 1988

The black man
thumped a watermelon

Pig feed, that's what it is
girl
you take it from an old
Texas melon man
this pile here ain't no good

WISHING ON THE AVON MOON

Cabin twenty's shower
runs hot
then cold

standing before the window
in summer nightgown
Maria brushes back her
mane of midnight hair

in which a migrant boy once
lost his way from Texas

fastens it with a Woolworth
clip
and makes a wish on the Avon moon

smells all its scents on her
rickety dresser

Evening Musk
Vivage
Fifth Avenue
and many more exotic names

Maria tells herself Avon should create
a brand new scent called
Rio Grande
to be worn by runaways

CHANGING DOLLS

Tony Bettencourt
never thought of chalk dolls
before he went to Vietnam

Too many live dolls
danced through the festas
of his valley years
nineteen of them

But now
he sells chalk dolls
at every swapmeet

hard cold ones
with painted faces

He cries when strangers
speak to him
asks them
do I know you

SATURDAY ESSENTIALS

E.B. went to Safeway
and the laundromat

A man's gotta eat
and wash his clothes
and have a little fun

dumped out his billfold
on the crumby motel bed

enough to see Loretta Lynn
at the fairgrounds
and buy a tank of gas

WHO ELSE

Who else but a raving
fool
would bring Grandpa to
Knotts Berry Farm, him 92
and only half a heart
just so he could visit
Judge Roy Bean's Saloon

and drink a toast of sarsaparilla
to Lily Langtry

RED IS FOR MARTYRS

This is a switch
I told myself when the priest
came out wearing red vestments
in honor of St. Matthew
the Martyr, Tax Collector

Candles flickered
I smote my chest
confessed my sins
and wished I had my taxes
back

the ones that paid to kill
the young men
in all our wars

A FATHER LAMENTING HIS DAUGHTER

The car was already
in the driveway

paunchy stricken Daddy
tried to console himself

It's not my fault
he told the walls

She wasn't raised to
take this route

but her mind is made up
you can see that

she's almost ready to leave
for the clinic

I don't know that it makes
any difference

but I wish to God
she wouldn't wear that
bright red dress

Black would be better
show more respect

WRITING POETRY ON NEW PAPER

Rich
alluring
this sudden change seems
sinful
too free and easy
for a Dustbowl woman

I must walk carefully
on good paper
one word at a time
feeling my way down a
new path
not yet realizing

there are no inky crossouts
no roadblocks
of junk mail flyers
to slow my pen

SPYING IN CITY PARK

My peanuts were gone
squirrels scampered away
and I saw a skinny young
couple in jeans
sit down on a park bench
near me

The boy put his arm across
the pale girl's shoulder
and told her seriously

You and me
ain't Romeo and Juliet
but we go together

The girl reached up
and touched his hand
and said
In olden times
they called this romance

and I need a Big Mac bad

THEATRICAL NAMES

Coming out of Colony Kitchen
in the Cherry Avenue Shopping Center
I hear a woman's voice call, Mitzi
and look ahead of me

I am thinking that Mitzi is a name for
actresses
at least two of them
Mitzi Green, child actress of my vintage
played Becky opposite Jackie Coogan in
Tom Sawyer about 1930
and Mitzi Gaynor, immortal as
Nellie Forbush in South Pacific

That name is not too common among us
cotton picking folks
We lean strongly toward Darla
Wanda Fay and Debbie Sue

WINGS

I walk toward the car
and see a woman has stopped beside
a giant truck and trailer rig
and is speaking to another woman
who is a new version of
the classic truck driver
young and trim in whipcord
shirt and trousers
wearing a cap with a visor

The first woman chides
Girl
are you ridin' alone in this big monster
The driver laughs
and the sound is music played on a line
of crystal glasses
She answers
No Ma'am
Merle Haggard rides with me
I pop a cassette into the tape deck
and we roll along the highway to Stockton
never a cross word between us

She adjusts her sunglasses
and climbs into the cab of the truck
She waves at the first woman and
slowly
carefully pulls out of the parking lot
past the midget cars
of lunchtime shoppers

and she has told the truth
about her travelling companion
as she passes me
I hear Merle Haggard singing
Silver Wings Shine in the Sunlight
Silver Wings
Carry You Away